EXPLORING EXETER

THE HEART OF THE CITY

JEAN MAUN

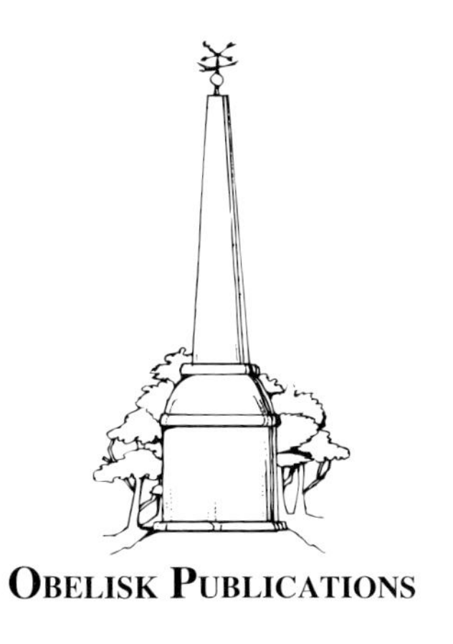

OBELISK PUBLICATIONS

Also By The Author
Exploring Exeter – The Quay
Exploring Exeter – The West Quarter

Other Titles of Interest
The Ghosts of Exeter, *Sally and Chips Barber*
The Lost City of Exeter – Revisited, *Chips Barber*
The Great Little Exeter Book, *Chips Barber*
Beautiful Exeter, *Chips Barber*
The Churches of Exeter, *Walter Jacobson*
An Exeter Boyhood, *Frank Retter*
Topsham Past and Present, *Chips Barber*
Topsham in Colour, *Chips Barber*
Pinhoe of Yesteryear, *Chips Barber*
Pinhoe of Yesteryear Part II, *Chips Barber*
Ide of Yesteryear, *Mavis Piller*
St Thomas of Yesteryear, Parts I, II and III, *Mavis Piller*
Whipton of Yesteryear, *Chips Barber & Don Lashbrook*

We have many other Devon titles, for a full list please send an SAE to Obelisk Publications, 2 Church Hill, Pinhoe, Exeter EX4 9ER or visit our website at www.ObeliskPublications.com

Acknowledgements
My thanks to my husband Ken, and son Howard, who checked my work and gave me encouragement to put my scripts for Iscatape into book form. I would also like to thank the staff of the West Country Studies Library for their help.

Plate Acknowledgements
All pictures by Chips and Andrea Barber
apart from page 19 (top) by Jean Maun

First published in 1996, reprinted in 2002 and 2010 by
Obelisk Publications, 2 Church Hill, Pinhoe, Exeter, Devon
Designed by Chips and Typeset by Sally Barber
Printed in Great Britain by
Short Run Press Ltd, Exeter, Devon

Introduction

Quite a few years ago I was approached by 'Iscatape' to make recordings describing various aspects and areas of Exeter. 'Iscatape' are a volunteer organisation, which produce and make available local news in an audio format, free of charge, for the blind and the partially sighted in Exeter. With news on one side and a magazine on the other, originally cassette tapes were posted to their clients once a fortnight, but now they have invested in memory sticks and players. Whilst working on the tapes, I researched various parts of Exeter, but I also received many requests for a written transcript. This little book is the result and deals with the 'Heart of Exeter', featuring many stories and much history from the area in and around the city centre. I hope that visitors and also locals will find something of interest in this historical trail, which never wanders too far from the High Street.

St Stephen's Church

Our walk starts in the High Street, outside St Stephen's Church. The Church is dedicated to the saint who was stoned to death for condemning the Jews for killing Jesus. He is the patron saint of Deacons, and his name is used to invoke a cure for headaches. Built of red Heavitree sandstone, the church has a small embattled tower with a turret characteristic of all Exeter's small churches, and an embattled north wall. Like the other inner-city churches, St Stephen's is a modest building with a very old foundation dating from before the coming of the Normans, and it is mentioned in the Domesday Book. The only part of the present building to date from this time is the crypt, revealed during restoration work in 1826, but filled in and sealed up again. Part of the church was rebuilt in the thirteenth century.

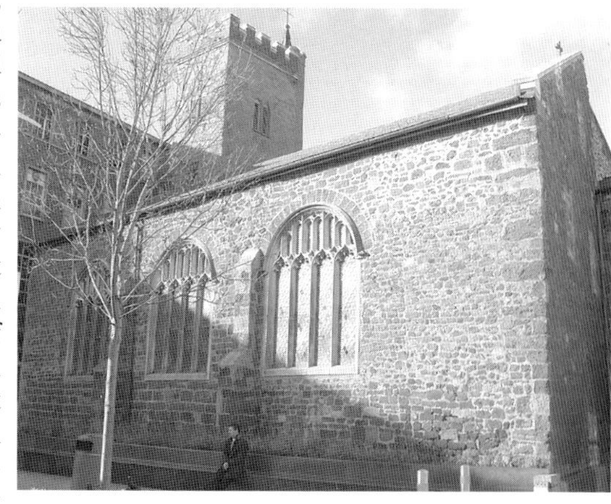

In Cromwell's time, the number of churches in Exeter was reduced to four, and St Stephen's was sold to a Toby Allen for £250, who used it as a stable, pulling down part of the tower. The church gradually fell into disrepair.

At the Restoration of the Monarchy in 1660 the parishioners recovered it and set about restoring it. However, during repairs it was totally destroyed by fire, but work again started and was completed in 1664. The present structure dates from this time, although the inside appearance was again altered in 1826 by the introduction of slender neo-Gothic quatrefoil columns. Because the church was made dim by the houses that crowded up against the South side, a sky light (which has since been removed) was added. Several times the church was threatened with demolition, and once it was mortgaged for £100.

In 1920 the newly formed University College of the South West, in nearby Gandy Street, increased the congregation so much that another door had to be cut at the north-east corner, which you can see on your left if you walk underneath the arch or bow beside the Church. In 1942 all the buildings around the church were destroyed by bombing, but the church sustained very little damage. An incendiary bomb set fire to the interior of the tower and caused the bells to fall and break up. The pieces were collected, and later sent to Whitechapel where they were recast into one new bell.

One of its most noteworthy features is the eastern bow, a raised chapel originally dedicated to St John the Baptist. At one time this was visible from the body of the church, and approached by a flight of ten steps through an open arch. The bow was rendered unsafe, so the 1664 Holy Table was brought forward, and the stairs blocked. It is now used as a meeting room. Above this entrance to the church is the Stuart Royal Coat of Arms of Charles II, and displayed on the north-east wall is a second Royal Coat of Arms of the Hanoverians. At the back of the Church was a gallery, the line of which is still visible over the vestry and porch.

In the vestry is a memorial to William Jackson, composer and organist of the Cathedral in 1777. He is remembered also for being told by Handel, "If you can't sing, keep your mouth open and look as if you are singing." The church has beautiful windows containing old stone tracery. The oldest memorial is to George Potter, a merchant of the city who died in 1662. He helped to rebuild the church. The tapestry was woven by Bobby Cox, wife of the Principal of Dartington College, near Totnes.

One interesting member of the congregation in the early nineteenth century was the Exeter embalmer, Mr Luscombe. He embalmed, at the Royal Clarence Hotel in the Cathedral Yard, Queen Victoria's father, the Duke of Kent, who had died when staying at Sidmouth.

Not many people live in the heart of the city, but the inner-city churches still have their uses in the service of God. St. Stephen's is used for many purposes. Flag Day organisers use it as their base; many coffee mornings are held in support of charitable causes; and lunchtime discussions take place there. Small orchestral and choral groups find the acoustics perfect for their concerts and some services are still held there.

The High Street Mural

Looking across the High Street we can see a store with a very wide pavement in front of it. This pavement narrows in front of the next shop on the left. Before 1991 this had a huge blank wall facing up the High Street, but the City Council have greatly improved this. They commissioned an artist to paint a mural on the wall, and this was done in September 1991. The resulting picture, which covers the whole wall, depicts the front of a Tudor house, complete with painted windows and doors, and a balcony in the top left hand corner with three figures looking down on modern Exeter.

A Man of Books

One of the men is Sir Thomas Bodley, who was born in 1544 in a house on or near this site, the eldest child of a family of twelve. When Mary came to the throne, the family escaped to Germany as his father hated Catholicism. They later moved to Geneva where Thomas, at the age of twelve, was sent to continue his studies, and he was tutored by some of the great scholars of the time. The family longed for their native country, so, when Elizabeth succeeded her sister as Queen, they returned to England and went to live in London. Thomas was awarded his B.A. at Magdalen College, Oxford at the age of nineteen, and continued to live in Oxford taking various tutorial posts at some of the colleges. To enable him to travel abroad he obtained a licence from the Queen to do so and spent four years travelling the continent improving his mastery of many languages.

When he returned to England he became Gentleman-Usher to the Queen, and then he joined the Diplomatic service, having been unsuccessful in obtaining a seat in Parliament. In 1586 he married a rich widow from Totnes, who had seven children. His wooing of her was certainly unconventional. The widow, Mary Bell, had many admirers, and Thomas saw her when he was playing cards; he asked a friend to play his hand for him and rushed out to propose to her. He became Her Majesty's Ambassador to the Hague, but after seven years in this post he returned home tired of the intrigues of politics. This ended his diplomatic career, and King James duly knighted him.

While serving abroad he discovered how inadequate the Oxford Library was compared to the Continental ones, especially with respect to its lack of books for study. In 1597 he wrote to the Vice Chancellor of Oxford University announcing that he wished to endow and fund a new public library at Oxford, which now bears his name, The Bodleian Library. Having a very wealthy wife he was able to buy many collections of books, and he also received gifts of books from his friends, which he gave to the library. In 1602 the Dean and Chapter of Exeter Cathedral gave him ninety-two volumes including manuscripts presented to the Cathedral Library by Exeter's first bishop, Leofric. Bodley died in 1612, a year after his wife and, having no heirs, left something to his wife's children, and everything else to the library.

The Miniature Painter

The second figure is Nicholas Hilliard, the great miniature painter, who was born in Exeter in 1547. It was said that the art of miniature painting in England began with him, as he had only a few predecessors who practised the art. He was the son of a jeweller who practised in Exeter, and his maternal grandfather was a goldsmith. His father, Richard, who was a Yorkshire man, was well known in Exeter as, in 1560 he held the post of High Sheriff of the City and County of Exeter. Nicholas was a keen admirer of Hans Holbein the younger, and developed his craft by studying his work. He painted a miniature of Mary Queen of Scots when he was only eighteen, and eventually set up business in Gutter Lane in London because he wished to secure work from noblemen at Court. He painted many court ladies, and also made fine pieces of accessories of jewellery for the royal court. His most famous work is the Armada Jewel, dated 1580. It is a miniature of Queen Elizabeth I set in a frame of enamelled gold, and studded with diamonds and rubies, showing his skill as a jeweller and goldsmith as well as a miniaturist. It was sold at Christies in 1935 for £2,835, when it was bought for The Royal Victoria and Albert Museum in London. He died in 1619, but left a son Laurence, who had been taught by his father. Hilliard's royal patronage, granted to him two years before, was passed to Laurence.

The Unlucky Princess

The third figure of a lady, is Princess Henrietta, youngest daughter of Charles I and Henrietta Maria. She was born in 1644 in Bedford House, the town house of the Earls of Bedford, which once stood on the site of the new Debenhams building. Charles I was being attacked by the Parliamentarians at Oxford, so he sent his Queen, who was also wanted as a traitor, to what was thought to be a safe Royalist stronghold, Exeter. She arrived here on May 1st, and on June 16th gave birth to a baby daughter. It was a difficult birth, and the Princess was left with her left shoulder higher than her right one. On July 21st the Princess was baptised in the Cathedral, but not at the present font. Richard Isaacke, in his memorials of the City of Exeter 1681, describes the ceremony thus: "In the body of the Church a font was erected on purpose under a rich canopy of state," and it is known that golden bowls were commonly used for royal baptisms. Later, in France, she adopted the second name Anne as a compliment to Anne of Austria. Charles I visited the Queen and Princess on July 26th, and stopped at Bedford House. He brought with him his eldest son Charles, who stayed at the Deanery. This was the last time the King saw the Queen and Princess.

Parliamentary forces were advancing into Devon, so Exeter was no longer a safe refuge for the Queen. Still in poor health, she left the City, and made her way via Falmouth to her native France. Charles placed Henrietta in the care of Sir John Berkeley and Lady Dalkeith, who showed her enormous devotion. Exeter was subsequently besieged by Fairfax, and a long siege began. Food became very scarce, when suddenly a large flock of larks fell on the city and was seized upon for sustenance. Eventually a surrender was negotiated by Berkeley, but although Parliament had undertaken to allow Henrietta and her guardian to reside where they wished, it forced them to go to Oatlands in Surrey. When the Parliamentarians wanted them to go to St James's Palace, where her brother and sister were detained, Lady Dalkeith dressed herself and the two-year-old Princess in rags, and with one attendant escaped to France, where they were reunited with the Queen. Henrietta grew up in France, often cold and hungry because her allowance from the French was sent to England to help the Royalist cause.

Charles I was captured and beheaded, and England came under the rule of the Protector Oliver Cromwell. After he died, his son Richard had no will to rule, so a strong man, General Monk, from Potheridge near Torrington, marched to London from Scotland. He sent agents to Prince Charles to return, and in 1660 Charles II was made King of England. General Monk also founded the Coldstream Guards, and there is a painting of him in our Guildhall.

Princess Henrietta eventually married Philip, Duke of Orleans and the only brother of the King of France. She had three children, two girls and a boy, but the boy died at the age of two. Her husband did his best to make her miserable. He preferred men's company to that of women, and was jealous of Henrietta's charm, intelligence and beauty, as she attracted many admirers including the King. Her position as sister of the King of England made her very important, and her letters to him gradually became more about State affairs than family matters. She was trusted by Charles and Louis, and became chief agent between the courts of France and England. In 1670 the Princess travelled to England to negotiate the Treaty of Dover, smoothing over the differences between the two countries after an outbreak of war in 1665. It is interesting to Devonians that this treaty was prepared by Sir Thomas Clifford, and the English version, in his own handwriting, is still preserved at Ugbrooke, near Chudleigh.

The Princess had never enjoyed good health, and after the signing of the treaty she returned to France to be suddenly taken ill with stomach pains. Within three days she was dead at the age of twenty-six. No one knows the cause: perhaps food poisoning or peritonitis caused by an ulcer. Some people believe she may have been poisoned by a very jealous husband, but there were no means to investigate such matters in those days. There is a portrait of Henrietta by Sir Peter Lely in our Guildhall, given to the City of Exeter by her brother Charles II, who often called her "A woman of Exeter".

The Old Houses in High Street

Progressing down the street, and standing with our backs to the House of Fraser store, we get an excellent view of three of the old Tudor houses overlooking High Street. The mural, which we have been viewing, is painted on the first of these, Number 229, but do not be deceived, because although it looks very old, and built in the Tudor style, it was, in fact, built in 1930 by a shoe company who demolished the Jacobean house that stood on the site. The oak interior of the old house was ripped out and shipped to America, and a new structure was erected on the site incorporating into the pseudo-seventeenth-century front two bay windows, one of which belonged to a demolished house in North Street. These match, and both have a wide Tudor-like black and white panelling beneath. A design of carved animals and humans on the black uprights appears to be holding the windows up, but both the windows oversail the road with no apparent support beneath them. As a typical merchant's house it was very deep along the side of Gandy Street, the narrow road adjoining it. Until the early nineteenth century it belonged to the Dean and Chapter. It was originally built of volcanic stone from Thorverton and red sandstone from Exeter. It is thought that Thomas Bodley lived here as a child, and that he may have even been born here. Over the centuries the house seems to have been occupied by a string of Mayors who each made their various alterations to the interior.

More Murals

Walking past the front of the building we can turn right and go a little way up Gandy Street and see on the side of the house a line of murals on boarded-up windows. In 1993 David Simpson was commissioned by the City Council and the Civic Society to paint them; except for the first one, they are copies of some of Nicholas Hilliard's miniatures. The first picture covers three panels, and depicts Thomas Bodley sitting in a library reading a book. The others cover one panel each, and are of Sir Walter Raleigh, Nicholas Hilliard (a self portrait), Richard Hilliard (father of Nicholas), and Sir Francis Drake. Other pictures have now been painted on the remaining boards.

Retracing our steps to the High Street and crossing to the opposite side, we can turn around and get a good view of the other houses in this group, which make such an attractive line of buildings along the street. Next to Gandy Street is a modern building, but number 227 follows, formerly known by Exonians as Ross's House. It was built about 1650 and belonged to woollen merchants John and Henry Weymouth. In the eighteenth century the City Council bought it and used it as judge's lodgings, which they had to supply for visiting circuit judges. It was also used for Mayoral functions before the Council sold it in the nineteenth century. A substantial part of the interior was then removed and parts of it were rebuilt. Then, in 1878 J. and G. Ross, outfitters, bought it, and hired builders to restore it under the guidance of a Dartmouth architect. He removed previous additions to the house, whilst retaining and repairing what was original.

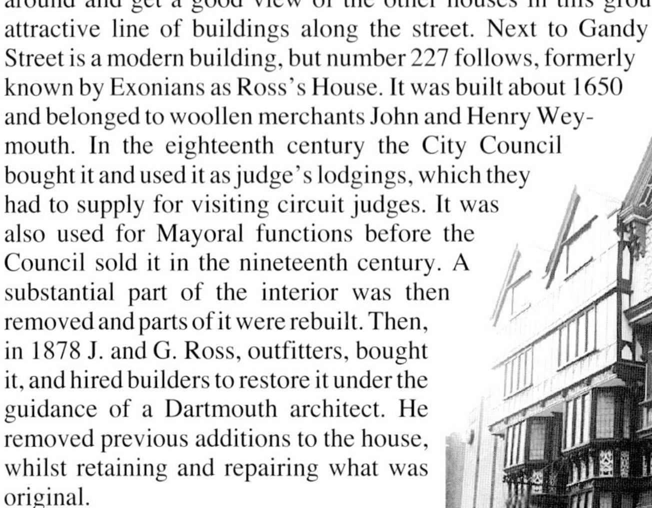

The façade was restored, and is largely original. On the first floor there are balustraded balconies either side of a beautiful mullioned and transomed window with a pediment over it containing a large coat of arms belonging to the guild of tailors. There are twelve small coats of arms in a line beneath it, all belonging to the various other guilds to be found in the city. The whole front of this floor has windows in it, but the side ones are difficult to see because of the balconies. The second floor consists of a row of attractive mullioned windows, with six black brackets supporting the floor above, which oversails it. The third floor consists of a four-arched gallery in the middle with a balustrade, probably original. It appears that this balcony may have gone the full width at one time, but it is now enclosed either side where closets were formed. The ends are finished off with a pinkish-white plaster with a kind of shell design all over it. Above this floor is a gable with a two-light window set in a wall decorated with overlapping tiles. This house is, I think, quite the most outstanding on the High Street.

Read All About It!

Next door numbers 223 and 225 have been converted into one building. They are five-storeyed timber-framed houses with gables facing the street, and were built in the sixteenth century by Thomas Prestwood, a wealthy merchant. In 1781 the house became the home and work place of Robert Trewman, printer and bookseller. Trewman's newspaper, the *Flying Post,* was printed here for eighty-one years, but newspapers continued to be printed here when the *Express and Echo* took over the premises, and 177 years of printing had been notched up when they moved out in 1958. The inside has been demolished and remodelled, and only the original Heavitree stone cellars remain. In the late 1950s it looked as if the houses would finally come down for road widening, but fortunately we still have them to add to the attractiveness of this corner.

Quite a lot of work was done on the façade. The ground, third and fourth floors were remodelled, while the first and second ones were cleaned and repaired, and are mostly original. These latter ones look so attractive with their mullioned and transomed windows set in dark oak, with the parts beside and beneath them decorated with a white geometric design. The second floor is oversailed by the third one, which has two mullioned and transomed windows set in a white wall decorated with vertical lines of dark oak, which continue on the fourth, or attic floor, which is divided into two gables, each with a small window. These upper floors oversail the ground floor, making the entrance appear rather dark. The oversailing is supported with three large carved animal brackets. There are a series of carved human and animal figures and moulded studs beneath the windows, and carved friezes and plaster panels beneath the first floor windows and between those of the first and second floors.

"Lift Up Thine Eyes"

Continuing our walk past the end of Queen Street, if we cross High Street and stand underneath Marks and Spencer's front we can look across to the other side of the street and see some equally old houses. Number 39/40 is a timber-framed building dating from the late seventeenth century. The brick façade was added in 1700, and there is very little left inside of the original features. The front hipped roof above the three-storeyed house, with a cock loft, is at right angles to the street.

Next door, numbers 41 and 42 were for years the premises of Hinton Lake the chemist, before Laura Ashley took over. These are a pair of twin-gabled merchants' houses, which have the date 1564 between the first-floor windows. Like their neighbour, they consist of three storeys and a cock loft, and under the ground floor are to be found Heavitree stone-lined cellars. The houses, converted into one, are tall, and are jettied out to gain maximum space. On the left of number 41 can be seen a stone wall separating it from number 40. This is a fire wall, and was built to prevent fire spreading from one house to the other, this being a real danger with timber-framed houses.

The next houses in the row are also very old, and make an odd addition to the High Street. The first and second ones have flat roofs, and both are two-storey houses. The third is very narrow and has two floors. The last two have only one window above the ground floor, and the last one looks like an infill.

Number 46 looks very old and is a three-storeyed house with an attic. The top storey is jettied out, and the coved second floor has vertical bands of spiralling beaded moulding of an ochre colour with angels on the corner which appear to support the upper floor.

Exeter's First Bishop

The houses which follow have been rebuilt and are in the modern style, until we come to 53 High Street, which belongs to Santander. The present façade, above the ground floor, was erected in 1907 when Boots the Chemist acquired the building. Mr Jesse Boot loved the Tudor style, and had many of his premises designed in it. The main timber structure of wainscot oak was shaped using the original Tudor method, without the aid of plane, sandpaper or varnish, at the company's workshops at Nottingham. In the centre of the second floor stands the statue of Leofric, Exeter's first Bishop, carved from a single butt of oak, designed by a London architect, and executed by Harry Hems, the great Exeter carver. It was hoisted into place in 1907 in the presence of Bishop Robertson. On the third floor can be seen, on the right above Leofric, his coat of arms, and on the left the arms of the diocese. On the first floor on the centre window can be seen the coat of arms of the city. The ground floor is very modern, while the first and second floors each have two windows surrounded with black and white panelling. The third floor has a small window above each coat of arms, and a flat central mullioned window. The whole top floor is gabled, and is white with black vertical timbers.

The Guildhall

Walking down the High Street towards the top of North Street we can see on the right hand side a rather large cream stone building with an open portico supported by four large pillars jutting half way across the pavement. The main pillars are made of granite and support the Mayor's Parlour on the first floor. The white carved upper part is of Beer Stone, and has pairs of columns separating the mullioned and transomed windows. The columns stand on a base, which has a frieze decorated with coats of arms. Above the parlour there are white railings, and well set back a roof of a further floor can be seen. This is the Guildhall, the oldest municipal building in England still in use, and there was probably some similar structure here even in Saxon times, as there is a reference to a *Guilthalla* on the site in 1160. I believe that, next to the Cathedral, it is our most important building.

The main part of the Guildhall dates from 1330; John Hooker refers to it having been built then, but it may not have been a completely new building. Over the centuries extensive work has been carried out on it, and in the fifteenth century the City Chamber was reconstructed and a new timber roof was made.

The portico was rebuilt in 1592, and the Guildhall as we see it today must be very similar to the one of that date. No further alterations have been made except for further internal re-arrangements during the seventeenth and eighteenth centuries.

In 1989 research was carried out into the history of the Guildhall, and it was discovered that the front was brightly coloured over many centuries. Small slivers of colour, found by Eddie Sinclair of the University, were analysed, resulting in a colour reconstruction of the façade. She said that the façade had been painted many times, and may have even been gilded. What a glorious sight that must have been in the centre of the main street. The whole of the front was cleaned in 1991.

Walking under the portico between the centre two pillars we can look up and see a large hook. No, this is *not* where they used to have the public hangings! During the last century street markets were held on Tuesdays and Fridays and the pork butchers' shambles stretched from Goldsmith Street to the Broadgate. The hook, at the centre arch, was for the suspension of the public scales provided by the City Chamber for weighing the meat. These were superintended by a staff bearer, and must have been a safeguard against unscrupulous traders. Under the hook there used to be a set of stocks which was used as a punishment for drunkards and people who committed minor offences. The punishment was to sit there for an hour or two, an open invitation for passers-by to pelt the offender with missiles.

The front has a set of railings across it with a gate in the middle. We walk through the opening and enter an outer hall by a modern wooden door with glass panels in it. This hall was where the city fire appliances used to be housed in earlier days. On the left is a room used by the Mace Sergeant. This was once the police station, and the twin room to it on the right was the Chief Constable's office. These rooms served this purpose for fifty years during the reign of Queen Victoria. In the Mace Sergeant's room is a trap door in the floor leading to cells beneath the Guildhall, which could also be entered from the basement of the Turk's Head next door. These cells were reputedly for holding men prisoners, while the females were accommodated at the rear of the premises.

The main hall has a beautiful large dark oak panelled Elizabethan door, which has a postern door in the middle, by which we enter. You have to remember to pick up your feet to step over the bottom ledge which is very deep, and also to duck your head as the opening is low. This was probably a safety precaution, so no one could attack the hall on horseback or go in two abreast brandishing swords.

Facing us as we enter is a beautiful stained-glass window covered with the coats of arms of Mayors and Receivers of the nineteenth century. On the left of this window, as you face it, is a large coat of arms of Elizabeth I and on the right the City coat of arms with *Semper Fidelis*, meaning 'always faithful', on it. This motto was given to the City by Elizabeth I for the part it played in the defeat of the Spanish Armada. On each side of the hall are more stained-glass windows containing names and dates of Receivers and Mayors of the City.

The main hall is lofty with a collar-and-brace ceiling, the main trusses of which rest on brackets which are made in the form of bears with a ragged staff, the emblem of the Earls of Warwick. They may have been put there in honour of Warwick the King Maker, who visited the city during the War of the Roses at the time when this roof was reconstructed. They are not very pretty animals. From the centre hangs a golden chandelier made by Thomas Pike of Bridgwater and brought here in 1789. Electric light has now been installed in it. The walls are oak-panelled, and inscribed on the lower parts are names and coats of arms of various holders of authority, trade guilds and benefactors, placed there in 1594. More have been added as the old ones have become worn. They were restored in 1887 by Robert Dymond. On the left of the hall is an open hearth, which has a large bust of Queen Victoria above it. Higher up on the walls are three paintings on either side, the most noteworthy being the first two on the right. The second is a full length portrait of Princess Henrietta, Duchess of Orleans (see page 6), painted by Lely, and given to the City by her brother Charles II. Lely also painted the first, of General Monk of Potheridge near Torrington, who was instrumental in bringing Charles II to the throne after the Commonwealth period. Thomas Hudson, a painter born in Exeter, painted two of the other portraits, the most noteworthy being that of Lord Chief Justice Pratt.

Opposite the door, and under the stained glass window, is a raised platform called The Hustings, erected in 1578 to raise the Mayor or judge above the rest of the court. On this platform is a large table and behind it a large chair in the middle with three smaller chairs either side. The seating in the body of the hall consists of long forms around the wall, which can be moved to the centre in a style very much like Parliament, some on the right, some on the left, and cross benches. The gallery above the door gives a good view of court or Council proceedings.

As we face this gallery we can see a staircase going up in the left hand corner, which leads to it and the Mayor's Parlour. This staircase is adorned with portraits, and at the top, turning right, we can see the City Regalia in glass cases. This includes Henry VII's sword and cap of maintenance, Nelson's sword, four Wait's chains, the City's chains of office and the City's silver. Opposite this is a painting by Northcote. It once depicted Napoleon on his horse Marengo, but the head of Napoleon was cut out and replaced by that of the Duke of Wellington. How the mighty fall!

By the side of the Regalia is a door which leads to the Mayor's Parlour, which at one time was a meeting place for the company of Merchant Adventurers, and in Victorian times it was used as the City Chamber. It became the Mayor's Parlour in 1901, and contains interesting china, furniture, silver and pictures. The room above the parlour was the Receiver's room, and in the late nineteenth century many valuable records and documents were found in this room and the one above.

The most important use of the Guildhall was as a court of law, and it is still used as a Magistrate's Court on Mondays. The City Council have their meetings here once a month, and it has always been used for official receptions, banquets, and meetings of voluntary groups. Being the centre of the town it was the place for proclamations to be read out, and even now the opening of the Lammas Fair is proclaimed here after the Mace Sergeant has carried a white glove on a white pole and hoisted it above the Guildhall for the duration of the Fair. Whenever Royalty have visited the City they have been entertained, by the Mayor, at the Guildhall, so it is still fully used throughout the year.

The Cathedral Close, Yard and Green

Martin's Lane

Retracing our steps along the High Street, for about eighty yards, we turn right opposite Queen Street into the very old Martin's Lane, typical of the streets in Exeter in the Middle Ages. We immediately get a whiff of beer, and soon come across the Ship Inn on the left hand side, a quaint Elizabethan building of plaster and dark oak façade, with low doorways and ceilings. This hostelry had a full face lift and interior renovations in 1994.

In the sixteenth century, the great Sir Francis Drake visited Exeter often, and the Shippe was where he met with many famous Devonians. In a letter, which he wrote in 1587, Drake said of the inn, "Next to mine own shippe I do most love that old Shippe in Exon, a tavern in Fyssh Street, as the people do call it, or as the Clergy will have it, St Martin's Lane."

The old Shippe played a part in the Civil War too; whilst Exeter was being besieged by the Roundhead Fairfax, Cavalier Captain Benet quartered his men there as it had excellent food and drink. It still does!

In 1710 a mob tried to burn it down as they thought that some of the Whig-sponsored clergy were staying there, and these were very unpopular. What a chequered history the building has had.

Walking farther down the lane we pass on the left what was, for many years, the SPCK bookshop, two converted gabled houses which once belonged to the Dean and Chapter and housed the Vicars of the Cathedral. There were others along Catherine Street but alas, these were demolished in the Second World War during the Blitz in 1942.

St Martin's Church

Past the entrance to Catherine Street is one of Exeter's inner city churches, dedicated to St Martin of Tours, the patron saint of drinkers and beggars. The original church was one of the oldest in Exeter, and was dedicated by Exeter's first Bishop, Leofric, in 1065. Alas this is not the same building as the old one was replaced in the fifteenth century by one built of local Heavitree stone, a red coloured sandstone. There were also additions made to it in the seventeenth and eighteenth centuries, when it was discovered that the new tower was not on St Martin's property, but that of the Dean and Chapter. A rental of four old pence a year had to be paid to the Cathedral for this mistake until 1931, when it was allowed to lapse. St Martin's has an irregular ground plan in that the direction of the nave differs slightly from that of the Chancel. I have been given two reasons for this, the first being that it represents Christ on the cross with his head bent. The second is that in mediaeval times the people were very superstitious and built their churches thus so that the Devil could not make a straight run at the Altar.

Mol's Coffee House

Walking a little towards the Cathedral, and standing on the cobbles, we can turn around and see what I believe to be the most photographed house in Exeter, known by Exonians as Mol's Coffee House. It is a beautiful building of the Tudor style with its transomed and mullioned bay windows on the first floor resembling the stern of an old English galleon. The many panes of glass are all of irregular shapes and differ slightly in size. It is said that Sir Francis Drake met his fellow admirals behind these windows in the room on the first floor, to plan the attack in 1588 on the Spanish Armada. This room is beautifully panelled in oak, and has a frieze displaying forty-six coats of arms of local people who either contributed money or ships or sailed with Drake during the Armada. The floor above this one has bow windows either side of a huge coat of arms of Elizabeth I with the date 1596 on it, and the name Mol's under it. The house was called Mol's as an Italian named Mol lived in or near it in the 1500s. The third floor has a balcony oversailing the floor beneath, and three windows, the middle one being a casement. Further up is a quaint Dutch gable, which was added at the beginning of the twentieth century.

This building is part of what was a larger one erected in 1529 to house the Annuellar Priests. It was the duty of these priests to pray for the souls of those departed who had left an annuity for them to do so. They would do this in a chapel in the Cathedral, on the anniversary of the death of the departed. These chantry priests only lasted for about twenty years as the Reformation soon put a stop to this practice. In 1549 the house was leased from the Dean and Chapter by a Richard Weston when it was subdivided. Although it is always known as Mol's Coffee House, coffee had not 'filtered' through at this date, and it is thought that maybe it became a coffee subscription house in the eighteenth century. At the end of the nineteenth century Mol's had become Mr Worth's Art Gallery, and the Dutch gable was then added to the third floor to give extra space for picture framing. However, when the first pictures were framed it was discovered that they could not be negotiated down the narrow twisty stairs. Sections of the floors were removed and pictures lowered down to the shop by means of ropes and pulleys.

The Statue of Richard Hooker

Moving away from the cobbles towards the grass of the Green we cannot miss the statue of Richard Hooker, at one time surrounded by prickly ground cover, but now by railings. The statue is of white Purbeck marble on a Devonshire granite pedestal, and stands on the ancient burial ground of the Cathedral Green. It is by Alfred Drury, and was presented to the Cathedral in 1907 by one of Hooker's descendants, and unveiled by the then bishop, Bishop Robertson. Richard Hooker, nephew of John Hooker, a chamberlain of the city, was born in 1553 at Heavitree in Exeter. After his early education at the Exeter Grammar school, under the patronage of his uncle and John Jewel, the Bishop of Salisbury, he entered Corpus Christi College, Oxford, and lectured there for several years after receiving his master's degree. In 1588, while living in London, and being a meek and modest divine, he was encouraged by his landlady to marry her daughter, reputedly a sharp-tongued bullying woman. In 1591 he became a minister at Boscombe, and a Prebendary at Salisbury Cathedral, although he still lived in his father-in-law's house in London. In 1595 he was made Rector of Bishopsbourne near Canterbury; after his death in 1600 he was buried there. He wrote many books, the most famous of which was eight volumes entitled *Of the Laws of Ecclesiastical Polity*, the last three volumes being published after his death. All eight volumes are important in Theology as they set down the basis for the Anglican Religion. It is said that he caught a fatal cold while travelling from London to Gravesend. One of the former Canons of the Cathedral said of the Statue, "There sits Hooker, alone on his perch, facing the pub, with his back to the Church."

The Royal Clarence Hotel

Turning completely around we can see that the aforementioned pub is the Royal Clarence Hotel, the large cream building in front of us. It was built in 1769 by William Praed, a banker of the City, on the site of a former house, the town house of the Raleigh family, who lived at Hayes Barton, East Budleigh. The main large part of the hotel was built as the city's Assembly Rooms, while the part on the right, which has iron balconies on the first floor, was his bank, and was, indeed, the first Exeter Bank. Eventually a Frenchman, Pierre Berlon, converted the Assembly Rooms into an hotel, and this was the first building in England to be known by this name. The hotel had many famous visitors – Nelson came after the Battle of the Nile, had a Press Conference there, and received the Freedom of the City. A sword, now to be found in the Guildhall, was presented by him to the City.

The Duchess of Clarence stopped there while visiting her sailor husband at Plymouth, and allowed the hotel to be known as The Clarence Hotel. Due to a quirk of history the

Duke of Clarence became king, 'Sailor Bill', William IV, and the Duchess became Queen Adelaide. The hotel then became The Royal Clarence. Nicholas I, the future Czar of Russia, visited, as did the Duke of Kent, Queen Victoria's father. He came in 1802, and again in 1820, although he knew nothing of the latter visit; he died while stopping at his home in Sidmouth, and it was his body that was brought to the Royal Clarence to await embalming. The only embalmer in the district was one Mr Luscombe, and it is said that he could not be found until word got around that it would be a knighthood or 2,000 guineas to execute the work. He took the money!

The bank part of this building became the first Deller's cafe in 1905, and remained as such for eleven years. At one time it housed the first cocktail bar, the Zodiac, which served a cocktail called the Corpse Reviver, an apt name, as for many centuries the Cathedral Green was a huge burial ground. All those who died in the city had to be buried there unless they were members of a religious order. This ground became higher and higher until in 1637 Bishop Hall put a stop to the practice, and had a burial ground provided on the edge of the City called St Bartholomew, as it was 'opened' on St Bartholomew's Day.

It was in The Royal Clarence that meetings were held to discuss gas street lighting for Exeter. When the hotel was called by a previous name, the Cadogan Hotel, a lady from Crediton held a meeting concerning the education of all the deaf children in the area, which led to the eventual opening of a school for the deaf. It is also known that Sir Edwin Lutyens planned parts of Castle Drogo, the last castle to be built in England, while stopping at the Royal Clarence, and many plans on Royal Clarence notepaper are to be found at the castle.

The Well House

To the left of The Royal Clarence is the Well House, which has served many functions, including a book shop and, prior to that, Veitch's the seed merchants. From time immemorial it has been owned by the Dean and Chapter, and used by the Vicars Choral. During Norman times a hall was erected on the premises, but this was removed in the fifteenth century and replaced with a tenement. This was added to in the seventeenth century, and three top stories were built. This building is now part of the Royal Clarence, and it has a most interesting cellar where an original Roman well and bath can be seen as well as stone archways from later periods. The building was built on part of the Cathedral graveyard, and the well has a macabre guardian, a skeleton of a woman in a glass case immured in the wall. She is thought to be a victim of the Black Death. There is a Victorian notice above it saying, "Birth is the first step unto Death."

Along The Close

To continue our progress around this area we desert our position by Hooker's Statue and walk up the pavement by the wall which goes around the Close. It is better to walk here as the road along The Close is cobbled: painful to the feet if the soles of your shoes are thin, and also a hazard for walking as it is easy to trip up on the uneven surface.

Moving towards Southernhay along Cathedral Close we pass a café, and two other shops, all of which are late sixteenth-century timber-framed houses. The middle one was given a face-lift in the eighteenth century and the interiors of all of them have been altered.

Number 5 The Close, now a restaurant, is a very interesting building. The front facing the roadway was built in brick in the late seventeenth century, but at the rear there is an older stone building which was part of the Annuellars' College. Taking a walk up the pathway between numbers 4 and 5 we can see this house dating from various periods, which is on three sides of a courtyard. Until 1991 it housed the Exeter and County Club, which depended upon its membership for finance. It consisted of club rooms, which included a restaurant, bar and billiard rooms among them. Sadly, due to the poor economic climate it was forced to close. It has its very own ghosts, Martha the Nun and John the Monk who fell in love with each other. Rather than being walled up alive, the punishment for this terrible sin, they plunged down the well, in each other's arms. Their story is written down and was to be found framed in a glass display box hanging in the billiard room when the club was open. There is a very heavy black door to the yard, but you can peep through some bars at the top and see the courtyard with a pedestal in the middle, where there used to be a well, we are told. The club had a refectory with a mediaeval-arched stone entrance, and a fifteenth-century oak screen and stone fireplace.

Next door, Number 6, the house of the Precentor of the Cathedral, has an eighteenth century façade formed on the front of an older Heavitree stone house. It has two eighteenth century white pillars forming a porch, and was a typical Hall House which was later divided horizontally and vertically to form reasonably sized rooms.

Number 7 is another intriguing house, now the home of the Devon and Exeter Institution. The house was built in about 1500 and began its life as a residence of a Cathedral Canon. In 1634, the lease, still held by the Dean and Chapter, was handed over to the Parliamentary General, Sir William Waller, whose daughter married Sir William Courtenay of Powderham. This was a real teenage marriage, as the total of the ages of the Bride and Groom was thirty years. In 1662 the lease passed to the Courtenays, and the house remained in the family for the next 150 years, serving as the town house of the Earls of Devon. Most rich and influential families had town houses in which to entertain their friends from London and other distant places. It is said that the last of the family to own the house was by way of being a spendthrift and, although he had a very large income, he went bankrupt.

The lease was obtained from the Dean and Chapter for the Devon and Exeter Institution in 1813. The hall and kitchen were demolished – in their place, and on the courtyard, two lofty libraries, both with galleries, were built. These were lit by two domed lanterns, one of which you can see if you stand back a little and look towards the roof. The one at the rear is much larger. The rear of the house is sixteenth century with a decorated plaster ceiling, probably by John Abbott of Frithelstock, the celebrated plasterer who decorated the ceiling of the Custom House on the Quay. The libraries have over 40,000 books, many of which cover the history and geography of the West Country. It also has copies of local newspapers dating from the 1700s.

In 1972 the day-to-day running of the library was taken over by the University. The club provides facilities for its members, who pay an annual subscription. The front of the building is of Heavitree stone, but it has white boarding panelled with black at the top with a sundial in the middle over the door. The sundial was put there to ensure that the clock in the hall was always correct. The panelling is an interesting feature. The rooms overlooking The Close on the first floor were to be used as reading rooms for the members. These, however, proved to be too dark as the windows were small and the ceilings were low. The roof was raised to give longer windows and higher rooms, and the boards on the top cover the stonework which fills the gap between the top of the walls and the new roof. The Institution also houses the headquarters of the Devonshire Association, the Devon and Cornwall Record Society, the Exeter Literary Society, the Civic Society and other local organisations. It acted as a weather station from 1818 to 1974, and has the only continuous weather records for the city for those years.

Numbers 8, 9 and 9A date from the sixteenth century, and then formed a single residence ranged around a central courtyard. The Law Library can be found among these. Number 9 is now the home of the Treasurer of the Cathedral

Number 10, the home of the Bishop of Crediton, dates from the fourteenth century onwards, but most of it is from the sixteenth and seventeenth centuries. In the Middle Ages it was the house of the Archdeacons of Barnstaple and Totnes. As we take a walk between numbers 10 and 11 we pass on our left an attractive heavy oak-studded door, dating from 1600. It is carved in a fantastic cubed design with a fan top and is similar to the one at the Guildhall. There is a small postern door in this large one, by which pedestrians would have entered, if carriages were not expected and the large door was shut. It is about 5 feet tall and $2^1/_2$ feet wide and has a deep step, so it is a kind of safety door barring the way against any intruder. Above it is Bishop Cotton's coat of arms. This front part of the building probably contained the stables. Walking farther in we come to a beautiful cobbled courtyard, a haven of peace in the middle of the busy city, which is a picture, especially when the wisteria is in full bloom. This covers one part of number 10, the Bishop's Chapel in the corner, and a side of number 11, the home of the Organist of the Cathedral, on the right. A little door stands opposite the entrance with Bishop Oldham's coat of arms over it. Bishop Oldham founded the Manchester Grammar School and, with his friend Bishop Fox, co-founded Corpus Christi College, Oxford. There are three owls on Bishop Oldham's coat of arms thought to be a play on the name Oldham, Owl-dom. There is a chapel dedicated to Bishop Oldham in the south choir aisle in the Cathedral, which has many owls around it. An old pump can be seen in front of the Organist's house, and there are also other plants to be found in small gardens and planters.

The Canada Connection

Walking out of the peaceful courtyard and turning left we come to Number 12 The Close, once the house of the Archdeacon of Exeter, now a Canon's residence. It was reconstructed in Heavitree stone after the Second World War as it had been demolished by bombs. This has a plaque on the front saying that in a house near this site John Graves Simcoe, the first Governor General of Upper Canada, now Ontario, lived as a boy. A little bit of Canada still remains in Devon at Wolford Chapel, near Honiton, where Simcoe was buried, and there you can see the Canadian flag flying.

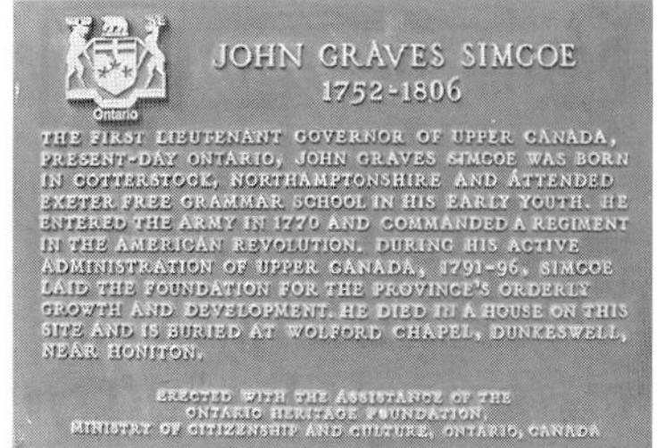

Opposite the Archdeacon's house is Hall House, part of the Cathedral School, named after Bishop Hall. This is the home of the Headmaster of the school, and some of the boys are boarded here.

Across the Cathedral Green

We now retrace our steps a little and walk across the grass with the Cathedral on our left. Pausing a little to look at the massive Norman North Tower we can see the outline of the apex of a house on the stone work. This is the mark showing the site of the Treasurer's house, and who knows, we may at this moment be standing in his parlour! Here Henry VII stood in 1497 and viewed the followers of Perkin Warbeck, pretender to the throne, through a newly cut window. There were sixteen massive trees on the green, and Henry ordered eight of them to be felled so that he could view the men better. He felt so sorry for the poor bedraggled crowd with halters around their necks that he forgave them, and they all went away shouting "God save the King." Not so Perkin Warbeck though, who was taken back to London and eventually executed.

Farther along we pass the North Door, which is the exit if you visit the Cathedral. Standing back a little to get a better view we can see the door, a modern glass one with the Diocesan cross keys and sword on a glass panel above it. There is an inner door, which is of heavy dark oak and very old. On either side of the door and above it there are ornate pointed triangular stonework pieces making a border around three alcoves. These were empty until the end of the First World War, after which Canon Stevens, of the Cathedral, had placed in them statues of patron saints of some of our allies, in thanksgiving for the safe return of his sons who fought in the war. Between the points at the top of the porch can be seen four windows on either side belonging to the Dog Whipper's room. In mediaeval times seats were not put out in the nave of the Cathedral, and hence there were always people and even animals milling around inside. The Dog Whipper's job was to make a path between the people for processions to the many services in the choir for the clergy only. He also had to drive the dogs out. There are two windows from this room looking into the Cathedral so that he could get a good view of the nave to make sure that all was well. The room is a kind of flat which has an upstairs and downstairs, and even a garderobe, or mediaeval toilet. You could say 'en suite facilities'.

Walking on, at the end of the grass and path we come to the square in front of the Cathedral. This is covered with granite sets, and leading to it is the main processional way to the Cathedral, a series of shallow steps which lead us to the site of the former Broadgate.

The Broadgate

Walking up some of these steps we find ourselves facing the Broadgate, with Cathedral Yard's mainly eighteenth and nineteenth century buildings on our right, and Tinley's next to the Broadgate. Tinley's was built in 1825 when the Broadgate was demolished, although some parts of the house date from the sixteenth century. Although it has had several changes of ownership since Mrs Tinley opened her tearooms in 1930, the name is still emblazoned across the top of the building.

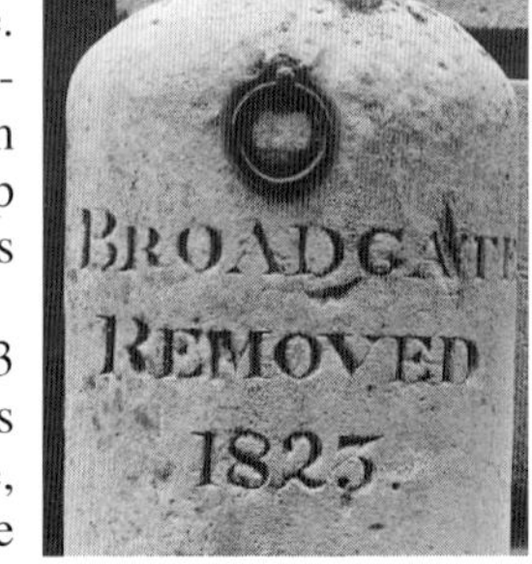

The need for gates around the Close came about in 1283 when a Precentor of the Cathedral, Walter Lechlade, was murdered on his way back from the Cathedral to his house, The Chantry, at 2 a.m. after Matins. The Chantry stood on the present site of the Cathedral School. No one could find the culprit, although there was a lot of bad feeling between the Bishop and the Dean and Mayor of the city, and although the vicars of Ottery and St Thomas were implicated nothing was ever proved against them. In 1285 Bishop Quival, in desperation, appealed to the king, Edward I to preside over a court case of the twenty-one people thought to have something to do with the murder. This number included the Mayor, the Dean and the keeper of the South Gate, which was found left open. The trial was on Christmas Eve, but the King decided to delay his summing up and sentencing until Boxing Day. Maybe he had a good Christmas, but I'm willing to bet the prisoners did not. On Boxing Day the Mayor and the keeper of the South Gate were sentenced to death, but the Dean pleaded privilege of clergy and was imprisoned in the Bishop's prison for a year, after which he repented and was set free. After the trial the Bishop requested that the Close should have a wall built around it with seven gates for access, the Broadgate being the main one. If you go into Tinley's, or the Royal Clarence you can still see part of the wall. A curfew was rung every night after dusk, when the gates were locked and all fires had to be doused. Remember, in those days all the houses were timber-framed and susceptible to fire. When the Cathedral closes, this curfew is still rung on the six and a quarter ton Peter Bell housed in the North Tower, which rings the number of times there are days in the current month. The Peter Bell was given to the Cathedral by Bishop Peter Courtenay, and it was so big that the North Tower had to be raised to accommodate it.

A Corner of the Cathedral Yard

Opposite the Broadgate, set on the grass, is the Devon County War Memorial. It is of Dartmoor granite, designed by Sir Edwin Lutyens, and commemorates the fallen of the two world wars. It is interesting to see the First World War dated on it as 1914 to 1919; this is because we still had troops on the Russian front until 1919.

Next to the old 'City Bank' established in 1786, is St Petrock's church, dedicated to a sixth century Welsh saint. This church was enlarged by building towards the Yard, and the nave does not run true east–west. One of the pedestrian gates went through the building to the High Street. It has six bells, five in the tower and the sixth one in the louvred part above the tower. It is one of the lightest peals in the country and of much interest to visiting campanologists. The church has the oldest complete church records in the country, dating from the twelfth century. Great re-arrangements were made to the interior of this building in 1994 to enable it to be made into a homeless centre. Originally run entirely by volunteers, but now with additional paid staff, the charity aims to support and encourage the homeless to improve their circumstances and take more control of their lives. Since its inception, they have helped over 9,000 people in the first 15 years.

Walking around the corner we can see the top of South Street, but we turn left and see in front of us, opposite St Petrock's, three tall gabled houses built in 1540 to house the craftsmen of the Cathedral. The size of these shows that these workers were held in very high esteem. Tudor door and window surrounds can still be seen on the middle of these three.

We now get a magnificent view of Exeter's Decorated Gothic Cathedral. Standing on the grass looking at it we are on the site of St Mary Major Church. It was decided to take this church down in 1971 as it was used very little; underneath, archeologists found evidence of a Roman bath house. There were also signs of the foundations of the Saxon Church built by Athelstan in 932, and this was probably the site of a monastery built in about 670, to which Boniface came from Crediton to be educated. Boniface eventually became the Apostle to the Germans after completing his education at Nursling. When he was in his seventies, he was killed by robbers at Dokkum in Holland.

This is altogether a very interesting site, as in 932 a Saxon church was founded here by Athelstan, but was burnt down by the Danes in 1004. A further one was built by Canute in 1019, which became Exeter's first Cathedral. Leofric, the ninth Bishop of Crediton, petitioned the Pope and Edward the Confessor to allow him to move his See to Exeter, as he considered a walled town a safer place to be in, and this was granted in 1050. This Church remained the Cathedral until William Warelwast, a nephew of William the Conqueror, became Bishop of Exeter. He desired a grander Cathedral befitting a great Norman, so the Norman Cathedral was started in about 1112, and dedicated on November 21st 1133, although it was not quite finished. The Norman Cathedral remained until the time of Bishop Bronescombe, who had seen Salisbury's Cathedral, and thought that Exeter should have a more decorated one. The present one was started between 1270 and 1280 at the Lady Chapel after a lot of foundation work had been executed along the south side which had been found to be sinking. Services still took place during the construction as a dividing screen was put up across the inside. The Altar was consecrated in 1328, and then the nave was started. The Cathedral was completed in 1369 by Bishop Grandisson. The two massive Norman towers were kept, and the stone work up to the window sills from the west end as far as the Bishop's Throne is Norman.

The West Front of the Cathedral

Looking at the West front we can see right at the top a statue of Saint Peter, the Patron Saint, naked and holding a fisherman's net by his feet. This is a direct reference from the Bible, John 21 verse 7. On either side of him there is a pinnacle. The one on our right is fairly new to this building. The original one was in a dangerous condition, and the whole of Devon was searched to find the matching stone. When making this one the stone masons put four faces around it at the bottom of the ornate carving: the Queen looking over the City, the Dean looking over the Deanery, a fisherman looking towards the sea and a farmer looking towards the land. Under a small window beneath Saint Peter is the Great West Window. There have been four windows glazed here, the first one being when the Cathedral was finished. It was re-glazed in the 1700s with Pecket glass. Pecket was a Yorkshireman, and a first-class stained-glass artist. It was re-glazed again in 1904 as a memorial to Archbishop Frederick Temple, who was once Bishop of Exeter. Interestingly his son, William, was born in Exeter, and he also became Archbishop of Canterbury. Sadly this glass was shattered during the bombing in the Second World War, but the window was re-glazed afterwards in the 1904 style. On either side of the window there is a pinnacle with a statue in a niche. On the left when you look at it is Athelstan who founded the first Cathedral, and on the right is Edward the Confessor, who installed the first Bishop. Under the West window is the image screen, an ornate structure beautifully carved in three tiers. The top tier shows disciples, apostles and ecclesiastics standing; the second depicts kings and warriors seated; and the bottom one has angels and demi-angels. On the right of the west door can be seen some windows between the image screen. These are the windows of Grandisson's Chapel, because it is where he was buried, and it is built within the thickness of the walls. Eddie Sinclair of the University has made an analysis of samples taken from the front of the Cathedral, and she says that these show that at one time it was a very brightly coloured building. Exeter Cathedral is unique as it has two Norman towers, north and south of the east end of the nave, making a cruciform ground plan; flying buttresses the full length to support the roof; and the longest unbroken Gothic vaulting in the world – over 300 feet.

The Cloisters

Walking towards the Cathedral and turning right when we reach the West Front, we can walk along until we reach some railings on our left. At the end of these there is a gate; if we turn left and enter it, we are in the Cloisters. The Cloister Walk was built in the fourteenth century, and if we look at the Cathedral on our left we can see the scars of this cloister walk on the buttresses. On the Cathedral between the buttresses we can see three round consecration marks, put there when this stage of the Cathedral was completed. Marks can also be seen on the Cathedral wall between the buttresses where six houses were built in the 1660s to house families down on their luck – a kind of 'grace and favour' housing. Glazing of the windows of the cloisters was done gradually, and on two occasions the cost of a window was imposed on a Canon as a fine for misbehaviour. When finished the cloisters surrounded four sides with an entrance porch. In 1448 the City Chamber wanted it opened, but the Dean complained of playing games, including 'tenys, by ungodly persons'. It would seem that nothing changes!

In 1661 the cloisters, in great need of repair after the Commonwealth period, were sold to the City Chamber. If we look to our right we can see black pillars between which the Chamber formed an open woollen market. A hall was built over it. In the nineteenth century the houses and cloth hall were pulled down and a project was started to reconstruct the cloisters. The plan was not carried out, although the Cloister Room was built in the right hand corner. In 1990 this was made into a refectory, and if we walk towards the Chapter House we see it on our right. The beautiful furniture inside was all made by the Cathedral carpenters, and a noteworthy feature of the place is the beautiful vaulting on the ceiling. A lovely place to have a coffee or a light meal.

The Chapter House

The Chapter House is in front of us. There is evidence that Bishop Brewer gave the land for it from his own garden in the thirteenth century to provide a place for the Dean and Chapter to carry out their business. In 1413 it was damaged by fire and the whole upper part had to be rebuilt. The first Dean, Serlo, was buried there. In 1421 Bishop Lacy had the roof altered, and the splendid ceiling is attributed to Bishop Bothe. In the time of Cromwell it was used as stables and a cloth hall was built in front of it. In the nineteenth century the cloth hall was removed and the Chapter House repaired.

Inside the building, and looking towards its east window, we can see modern sculptures set in arcades on either side. On the North side they depict scenes from the Creation, and on the South scenes from the Annunciation to Christ risen. They were made in 1974 in fibreglass and aluminium by Kenneth Carter.

The doors of the Chapter House are very interesting. If we look at them from the outside we can see a design like a Tudor rose on each door. Behind these are shutters which slide back and allow anyone inside to look out. When anyone is going to be installed to the foundation of the Cathedral (that is, anyone entitled to a seat, like a Canon) the procession starts from here. Everyone lines up and the Dean enquires of the Head Virger, "Will you ascertain if there are any contumacious persons without?" The Virger takes a peep to see if there are any persons outside up to no good, and then tells the Dean that all is clear, and the procession proceeds. This ritual dates from the murder of Lechlade.

A visit to the Cathedral is a must for everyone, and there you will find special facilities for the blind in the form of a scale model to feel, with a supporting tape describing the different parts of the Cathedral. There is also a tape with commentary to enable people to walk around the building with an escort, each hearing the commentary through a personal stereo. I could not begin to tell you all the fascinating things you will discover inside, so take a visit and see for yourself.

Towards the East of the City Centre

Catherine Street

Retracing our steps to Mol's, we exit the Close beside St Martin's church and walk up Catherine Street. This is quite a narrow street at the start, where we pass the pink Heavitree sandstone Oddfellows Hall on our right, and the modern House of Fraser on our left. After this point the street widens, and set back a few feet on the right we pass various shops and cafés. The building on the left is set back much further at this point, which gives an open square in the middle where the underground public toilets are situated.

Opposite are two ruined sites. The first is the remains of the Annuellars' College built in the sixteenth century, which extended to Mol's in the Close. This was built on the site of a fourteenth century mediaeval house, and on the left you can see the remains of a fireplace and oven. Under the foundations lay the remains of the first century Roman rampart, and the Council have put two posts about three feet high in the garden facing us at the back to show the position of a wooden tower belonging to this rampart. Before the War the Annuellars' College had been altered considerably and made into the Countryhouse Inn.

Next door are the remains of St Catherine's Almshouses and Chapel, now a mere shell outside, and only the walls of the Chapel in the middle, remain standing. These were once almshouses founded by Canon John Stevens in 1457 for thirteen poor men, supposed to represent Christ and the twelve Apostles. When Stevens died he handed over his charity to the Dean and Chapter. By 1536 the houses were occupied but the Chapel was disused. The order was suppressed by Edward VI and restored to the Dean and Chapter by Elizabeth I. At one time the Chapel was used as a carpenter's shop, and later was divided in two to provide accommodation for some old women. After that the buildings fell into disuse, but through the generosity of Lady Hulham of Exmouth, it was restored and passed to the Church Army in 1894. Captain Vic Call of the Church Army remembers the chopping of wood for fires, and the men living there selling it to householders in the city, the proceeds of which helped to keep the hostel going, and enabled the men to earn some money. Some were ex-prisoners from the County Gaol, who would save up their money to pay their train fare home. Up to the destruction, some of the accommodation was set aside for servicemen, and mobile canteens operated from here.

Both these sites were bombed in May 1942, and have been landscaped as a memorial to the citizens of Exeter who lost their lives in the Blitz. The City Council have placed seats around, and planted herbs here. Opposite this site is St Stephen's Church, where we started earlier.

Bedford Street

We continue along Catherine Street passing St Stephen's House on the left-hand side and find ourselves in Bedford Street. In pre-war times this led to Bedford Circus, an oval area comprising private houses, a chapel and gardens. Those who lived in Exeter before the Second World War must remember Deller's Café, the entrance of which was on the corner of Catherine Street, and which went over Lloyds Bank on the High Street. The street has been pedestrianized to create a square, which is ideal for street entertainment and outside café areas. Bedford Street has been incorporated within the Princesshay development.

Princesshay

After turning right and walking about thirty yards, then turning left and crossing the street, we are at Princesshay. This was one of the first purpose-built pedestrian precincts in the country. It was opened in October 1949 by Princess Elizabeth, three years before

she became Queen. A plaque commemorating the opening once stood within a walled seating area in the centre of the street. This precinct was demolished in 2005 and reopened following redevelopment two years later.

Walking along Princesshay we reach an arcade, leading to our left through to the High Street, and to our right to Roman Walk. If we look back at this point we can enjoy a lovely view of the Cathedral. High up on the façades of the two corner buildings stand two statues of women, named *Hope and Despair*. The one on the left holds aloft a flaming torch, signifying hope for the future, while the one on the right covers her face with her arm, denoting despair at the devastation the city suffered during the war. Further along Princesshay we come across another statue, the Blue Boy, which commemorates the medieval St John's Hospital School, which stood on this site. It was closed in 1931, then the premises were destroyed by bombing. My husband was a pupil at this school at the time it closed. The original school consisted of orphans, who wore a blue gown and lived in the building. In 1661 a high school occupied the top floor, with an elementary school on the ground floor. The high school later moved to Manston Terrace to become the Exeter School. Its first head was a Mr Nosworthy, who must have been buried there; his headstone was found in the rubble. It was subsequently moved to the Exeter School.

Just past the Blue Boy there was previously a fountain featuring a carving of the Cathedral in 1942 surrounded by rubble. The fountain

was laid in 1992 to mark the fiftieth anniversary of the bombing, but was dismantled during the redevelopment of Princesshay in 2005. If you turn right and take a short detour down Roman Walk, however, keeping the wall on your left, where the interruption of the wall leads to Southernhay, you can find the carving mounted on a large free-standing plaque. Retracing our footsteps back to the Blue Boy, we continue.

Eastgate

A line of red bricks leads from the tower of the city wall toward the High Street until a plaque on the wall, which marks the site of the East Gate. This path traces that taken by the old city wall. Again returning to the Blue Boy, continue along Princesshay. Behind the tower at the end of the city wall is the site occupied by the Giraffe café, which was subject to an attempted terrorist bombing in 2008. Continuing further along we reach Paris Street; and if we turn to the left, we see the entrance to the underground passages.

Underground Passages

The earliest underground passage was cut in the twelfth century by the Cathedral authorities. It was bored through the ridge of the East Gate to carry water from St Sidwell's Well down to the conduit in the Cathedral Close, and extended in the thirteenth century when the Dean and Chapter granted one-third of the supply to St Nicholas Priory. During the fourteenth century, pipes were laid, the alignment of the passages was altered, and a new aqueduct was cut; the conduit in the Close was encased in a structure and became known as St Peter's Conduit. The Dean and Chapter agreed to provide one third of this supply to a city conduit which was built at a point called The Carfax, at the intersection of North Street, South Street and Fore Street. The Cathedral required the Priory and the City to pay eight shillings a year for their share of the water, but this agreement was satisfactory to neither, and both sought separate supplies: the Priory laid pipes from a well in Paul Street, and a few years later the City established a new source of supply known as Headwell at Lions Halt. The water was carried down the Longbrook valley to enter the underground passages, and was then conveyed in lead pipes down the line of the High Street.

The tunnels are unusual because of their size and the distance they travel. There is a charge, but it is well worth a visit. At the start of a guided tour (and the passages have their own guides) you will first be shown a video about the history of the place. The guide will then lead you around the electrically lit passages. In parts of the tunnel the rock is exposed, but some are lined with local, volcanic trap of Heavitree sandstone, both of which gave off a pinkish hue. Only a few are accessible, and it is possible to stand upright most of the way – but then, I'm only five foot two! None of the lead pipes now survive, as in 1950 some labourers working on the road nearby broke into the passages and stole the remaining lead to melt it down. Sections of the passages still exist beneath the city, though they have been broken in places by the foundations of later development and by bombing during the war. In certain places you used to be able to smell the coffee that was being roasted in Carwardines of Princesshay, but now I understand you are more likely to smell bacon being cooked in a takeaway in Roman Walk.

Coming out of the underground passages we continue along Paris Street to what was formerly known as London Inn Square, at the top of the High Street. Turning into the High Street and looking right we can see a modern stone-coloured sculpture of a family. In 1989, to celebrate the Year of the Pedestrian, Devon County Council commissioned Cornish sculptor Carole Vincent to create four works, placed in Barnstaple, Torquay, Plymouth and Exeter. The sculpture features three adult figures at the back with two children in the front.

Turning right and walking a few paces back up the High Street there is an arcade with a fancy green metal canopy at the entrance: this is Roman Gate, which was opened in the late 1980s. Walking up this lane, about halfway along on the right we see the emergency exit of the underground passages. Through the window is an example of a very old fire engine, which was pulled along by the firemen!

Northernhay Place and Gardens

Coming to the end of Roman Gate we find ourselves opposite the end of Northernhay Place. In front of us to the left, on the site of a former medieval castle prison, we see the top of a building, which was originally a Methodist Church before the Royal British Legion took over. When the Legion wished to extend their premises, there was only one way to go – up – and so they literally 'raised the roof'!

We must now cross the road (carefully: the traffic seems to whiz around this corner) and proceed up Northernhay Place, which is flanked by Georgian houses and new offices, to the entrance of Northernhay Gardens. These gardens, which were originally opened as a public walk in 1612, are reputed to be the first public gardens in the country. The space was ruined during the Civil War, and restored 52 years later.

The entrance has two large wrought iron gates with Exeter's coat-of-arms on each one; just beyond which stands a masterpiece in bronze called *The Deer Stalker*. This sculpture, by the well-known Exeter sculptor E. B. Stephens, was presented to the citizens of the city by a number of his friends and admirers in 1878. There are several other sculptures throughout the gardens by local artists including John Angel and Harry Hems. As we walk along the path, rising above us to our left is the city wall, while to the right is the deep Longbrook valley. This deep escarpment topped by a high wall must have been a rear defence to this side of the city. The valley would have been even deeper before the brook running along was filled in; now it accommodates the railway line to Central Station, which was opened in 1861, the first railway having arrived in Exeter in 1844 when Brunel's line from Bristol reached the city.

Further along the path, to the right is the bandstand where concerts used to be held every Sunday afternoon; we take the path to the left, climb some steps and follow the wall around. Stopping for a breather at the top of the steps with our backs to the wall, in front of us we can see, across the valley, the Devon County Gaol, built in 1853. This gaol has one main claim to fame: the 'man they could not hang', John 'Babbacombe' Lee. John Lee was a young man in 1885 who worked for a lady in Babbacombe. One morning she was found murdered. John was arrested, tried and convicted, then sentenced to death by hanging. On the day of his execution he was taken to the gallows, but on each of the three occasions they tried to hang him, the trapdoor would not work. Eventually he was given a life sentence instead.

Behind the gaol the many buildings of the University of Exeter can be seen. These were constructed on the Streatham Estate, which was purchased in 1922, and includes Streatham Hall, which was renamed Reed Hall after Alderman Reed, who provided the purchase money. The first purpose-built building was the Washington Singer Laboratories, completed in 1922, and named after its benefactors, the Singer sewing-machine family. There has been ongoing construction since that date, and the University finally received its Charter in 1955. This university has one of the most beautiful campuses in the country.

Rougemont Gardens

Following the path up we come to Athelstan's Tower, the highest point in the city and within Rougemont Castle. It was built in the late twelfth century as a lookout tower by the Normans, and is wrongly ascribed to the Saxon king Athelstan. Walking through it we notice that it is a double tower with one part partitioned off by a large metal door. Walking around the corner we are now in Rougemont Gardens and get a splendid view of the surrounding area. Looking down from this high position we see the City War Memorial by Angel, a local artist. It is magnificent with a winged victory on the top, and

around the plinth figures of a soldier, sailor, nurse and prisoner. This was put here in the early 1920s to commemorate the victims of the First World War, and it is now also a memorial to victims of the Second World War. On Remembrance Sunday a short service is held here, and a bugler goes to the top of Athelstan's Tower and plays the Last Post. If the gate was locked, walk down to the memorial, and just to the left we find another route through. Either way, follow the path, skirting the dry moat of the castle on your right and the castle curtain wall on your left. This brings us down to Rougemont House.

Rougemont House was built in 1768 by John Patch, a surgeon of the city. His family had made their fortune in the service of the Stuart Kings in exile in France, and when he returned to England he leased this site from the Duchy of Cornwall to build a house. He was said to be a keen gardener, and the gardens, set in the moat of Rougemont Castle, owe much to his planning and enthusiasm. After his death the house was sold to Edmund Granger, a local wine merchant, who extended and altered the house in 1810. It was then one of the largest houses in the city. His successor was Richard Somers Gard, who made a fortune in share dealing, and who was a Member of Parliament for the city from 1857 to 1865. His widow continued to live here, and opened the grounds to the public. In 1912 the City Council purchased the estate, and in recent years the house has undergone a major face lift.

Opposite Rougemont House is the Rougemont Castle Gatehouse. This is the only remaining part of William the Conqueror's castle of 1068, and the oldest building like it in the country. Looking to the top there are two Saxon windows, so perhaps William used Exeter craftsmen to help him to build it. The structure is very high, and about one third of the way up is a ledge where probably the drawbridge started, although there was only ever a dry moat. Just above this is a large high Norman arched doorway, now closed up with stones. In front of the gatehouse there were once three small cannons, said to be from the Spanish Armada.

The Library

Turning right and keeping Rougemont House on the left, we walk down a slightly sloping path which veers to the left and goes in front of the house. Before the bend we can see in front of us the grassy banks of the old castle dry moat, on which children love to roly-poly down to the bottom. Glancing towards the front of the house we can see lovely wrought iron balconies of Regency design added to the Georgian building. The house is part of the museum, although not open to the public. Next to Rougemont House we pass the Westcountry Studies Library, where I get a lot of my information for guiding and my other interest, family history. These are housed in a building which, when built in 1936, housed the City Library which was burnt out in the Blitz in 1942. The building was a substantial brick one so the City was able to reuse it.

Past that, and attached to it, is the City Library, built in 1965, and opened by Princess Alexandra, the Architect being H. G. Rowe. Much of the design and putting together of the work was done by a friend of mine, Bill Chapple of Pinhoe, who was a leading Architect for the City Council. He tells me that their brief was to attach the new library to the old, and to do this they had to encroach on Rougemont ground. There was a large Cedar tree there which had to be left, so the library was designed in a curve to go around it. Building was well on the way, and the main structures in place, when filling in commenced. Bill said that one morning, after a very stormy night, an Irish worker came to him laughing his head off, to announce "The b***** tree's blown down!" It had indeed, but another was put in its place, which is on our right, and is now huge. On our left we can look into the children's library. Keeping to the path, which now veers to the right, we walk about 20 yards and take a small sloping path on our left which brings us into a small square beneath the front of the library, and we walk down the little alley in front of us, New Buildings. This is typical of alleys which crisscrossed Exeter from Mediaeval times, and it is shown on a map dated 1744. There is an exposed section of wall on our left giving an excellent example of the brick and timber method of construction, followed by small shops, and opposite there are also small shops. At the end we turn right into Gandy Street, once known as Curre Street when it was the centre for the leather workers.

Along Gandy Street

It is an ancient thoroughfare, which in the early eighteenth century was named after the Gandy family who were prominent in the City's civic life, providing seventeenth and eighteenth century mayors for the city. The street has been re-laid with granite sets in the mediaeval fashion with a central gutter, which in earlier times took water, slops, and other equally obnoxious substances. Turning right and walking along Gandy Street, we see in front of us the side of a large Victorian building, the Royal Albert Memorial Museum. As we approach it, there is a large opening on our right, Bradninch Place, with cars parked up the slope in front of another large building, once the University College of the South West, now the Phoenix Arts Centre.

Exeter's Royal Albert Museum

Soon after the death of the Prince Regent in 1861, a fund was launched to build a museum, and a site, the front part of the present building, was presented to the city by its MP, Richard Somers Gard, the same person who bought Rougemont House. The rest of the site was purchased for £2,000. Collections of exhibits started to be acquired, and were kept in a private gallery in Colleton Crescent. In 1864 an architect, John Haywood, was appointed. He drew up the plans for St Lukes College and the new gaol in New North Road. The building is in a Gothic design and mainly built of Pocombe stone, which is a darkish brick colour with a white vein in it. The foundation stone was laid in 1865 by Somers Gard, but it took longer than expected to build, and was further delayed by a major strike (so they had them in those days!).

However, the central area and the North Wing were completed in 1868, and opened with a grand bazaar and fancy dress ball, raising £3,000 for the funds. These areas were used for a Reference Library and School of Art. The South wing was completed in 1869, and School of Science classes were started here. The Museum was to be found on both floors alongside these. The City of Exeter and County of Devon had now gained the School of Science, which later became the University, the School of Art, later the Art College, the Free Public Library and the Museum integrated under one single roof, an idea which Prince Albert had favoured. Further extensions were made, and the last one was opened in 1899 by the Duke and Duchess of York (later George V and Queen Mary), and was granted the name Royal Albert Memorial. However, the School of Science, or college, soon needed additional space, and the large building set at the top of the slope in Bradninch Place was built, and this formed the University College of the South West. This was vacated by 1955, and the building is now the Arts Centre. Between 2007 and 2011 the museum was closed for a multi-million pound refurbishment.

Continuing to the end of the street, we turn left and walk down the short distance of Upper Paul Street to Queen Street, where we turn right and walk to the pelican crossing in front of the museum. Waiting to cross, and glancing to the left on the opposite side of the road, we can see the façade of the Higher Market

The Higher Market and Shopping Centres

For health reasons, after the cholera epidemic in 1832, there was a desire to close down all the street markets, and indoor markets were built to put stalls under cover. George Dymond was chosen to design it, but he tragically died young, and was replaced by Charles Fowler, a Devon man, who won the competition for building the Lower Market, which was later destroyed in the Blitz. He had completed the markets at Hungerford and Covent Garden, and won the competition for building the new London Bridge. The façade, mainly Dymond's design, has Doric pillars, and a portico faced with soft cream Bath stone. Originally the market served fish, poultry, dairy and vegetable produce, and within the centre was the Civic Hall. By 1962 these had moved elsewhere, and the market closed down. There were demands to demolish it, but instead it became part of the busy Guildhall Shopping Centre.

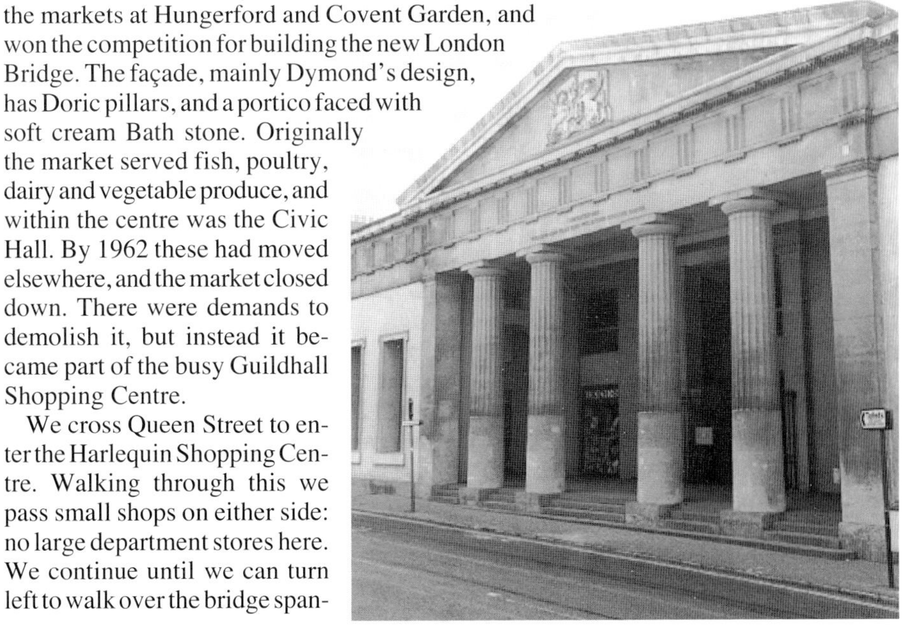

We cross Queen Street to enter the Harlequin Shopping Centre. Walking through this we pass small shops on either side: no large department stores here. We continue until we can turn left to walk over the bridge spanning Paul Street, and approach the Guildhall Shopping Centre. On the right is Primark, and towards the end opposite this is a ceramic wall plaque. This, read from bottom to top tells some of the history of Exeter, with pictures of Roman artifacts, a tillet block, mediaeval houses, the Guildhall, the Higher Market, the Cathedral, and right at the top, the countryside.

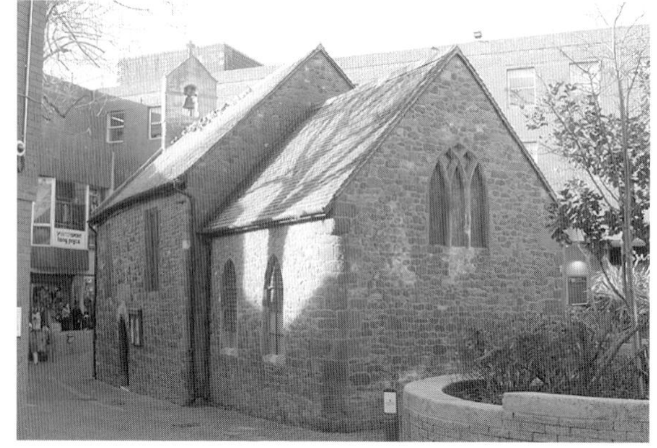

About twenty yards ahead we see the eleventh-century St Pancras Church, dedicated to a fourth century Roman saint who was martyred at the age of fourteen. What he had done in those few years to receive this punishment no one knows. This is one of the churches of the Parish of Central Exeter, and is no longer used for regular services but as a Third World centre. It has one small bell which has the inscription 'I may be small but I can be heard afar'.

Walking past with the church on our left we approach the back of the Guildhall, and are now standing in Waterbeer Street, the street of the waterbearers. In mediaeval times water used to be transported from the river to this street to be sold for a ha'penny a bucket or three buckets a penny. At the rear of the Guildhall in front of us we can see on the ground floor small barred windows where the female prisoners were kept in cells, and the windows above are those of the jury room. I won't say any more about the Guildhall, as I have already covered that in detail. On our left we can see the cream pillars of Marks and Spencer, reconstructed to the same design as the previous building, Waltons. Earlier than that there was a woollen hall here.

We turn right and walk down Waterbeer Street, past the wide entrance to High Street, and find on our left a very narrow street called Parliament Street, reputed to be the smallest street in the world. If you are very large you will find difficulty in walking right through as it gets extremely narrow at the High Street end. City Guides have to be careful not to take people pushing wide pushchairs through here.

At the end of it we step from the shadow of the high buildings into the brightness of High Street and the end of this historic trail, just about a hundred yards from where we began.